Vignettes - rhymes and stories from the valley

Andrew Grundon

BookLeaf Publishing

India | USA | UK

Presentation by *BookLeaf Publishing*

Web: www.bookleafpub.com

E-mail: info@bookleafpub.com

ISBN: 9789358318913

First edition 2024

To my daughter, who is my life and my inspiration always.

ACKNOWLEDGEMENT

This book, and indeed my entire life spent in artistic pursuits, could never happen without the support and tolerance of family and friends.
Many times when I have doubted myself they have not.
When I have been absorbed in my work and neglected them, they have forgiven me.
Thank you, from the bottom of my heart.

PREFACE

Welcome.
Pull up a chair.

Autumn

Confetti showers of russet and auburn
torn from the frost-numbed fingers of trees
Orange and ochre, the dry tears of autumn
dancing away on the stiffening breeze.

Brown paper flurries of gold flecked with copper
blown into drifts in the porch by the door
Swirling around as we step 'cross the threshold
coming to rest on the earthenware floor.

Shut out the gloaming and hang up your raincoat
I'll feed the stove while you pull up a chair.
Sit for a while, and please join me in toasting
the shortening days and the chill in the air.

The artist

Shackled by self-doubt, but aching to create
He is besieged by a manic euphoric desperation.
Left raw from the endless grappling with his
demons and muses
He is exquisitely, agonisingly sensitive
And every subtle nuance of atmosphere
Becomes a dazzling kaleidoscope of intense
hues.
Be gentle with him
Forgive him
He is an artist
And by his hand
even the most mean-spirited among us
can be bewitched and enriched
And through his eyes
we can glimpse eternity.

Brown

It must be nigh on fifty years since I first met the bear
In a little Yorkshire toyshop, in the corner by the stairs.

Outside was damp and dingy but the lights inside the store
Made everything feel cosy as we bustled through the door.

It seemed we'd walked for miles in the rain that afternoon.
We didn't have much time to browse, the shop was shutting soon.

But when I saw his little face gaze at me from the shelf
He was the only plaything that I wanted for myself

Something inside me melted and I knew I had to own
That simple little brown bear, I had to take him home.

I just had enough pennies if I spent all that I had
But all my pocket money I would use up and be
glad.

My parents wouldn't let me, though I begged til
I was sore
Reluctantly I put him back and stroked his little
paw.

Zipped up inside my parka and staring at the
ground
My heart in bits from losing what had only just
been found.

My father swore emphatically I couldn't go back
there
But I saw my mother weakening for she too
loved the bear.

Trying to be angry she stopped there in the street
Looked into my tear-streaked face and knew that
she was beat.

She and I half ran back down to where the little
shop
Was being locked up for the night, and begged
the man to stop

I hardly dared to look upon the shelf beside the
stairs
Afraid that I was going to find the little bear not
there.

But here he was just where he'd been. I took him
in my arms
And clutching all my pennies in my soaking,
shaking palm
I placed him on the counter beside the old shop
till
And gave the man my fortune. I remember his
smile still.

He offered me a paper bag to keep my brown
bear dry
But I tucked him deep inside my coat, so happy I
could cry.

I don't recall the walk back much, that wet day
in September
My heart was full of love and joy, that much I
can remember.

Throughout my youth we moved a lot, all up and
down the nation
My dad was in the R.A.F. ,we went where he
was stationed.

In each new place we'd start again we never had
a home
You never seem to put down roots when all you
do is roam.

But every night throughout it all when I laid
down my head
My little brown bear teddy would be snuggled in
my bed.
For he was always constant, my comfort in the
night
And when the world was darkest he made
everything alright.

Decades have passed and now at last I find that I
have grown.
I have a home, stability and family of my own,
Although I've outgrown childish things and left
all that behind,
Abandoning my childhood friend would just feel
too unkind.

If you looked into my bedroom, by the window
there's a chest
It's still home to a small Brown Bear
The friend who knows me best.

Stove

This morning feels like Autumn.
A petulant wind gusts
around and through
the tired wisteria
framing the front window.
Rain sputters fitfully against the glass,
and a keen chill seasons the air
with an unmistakable taint of change
that hangs ominous and exciting
in the half light.

The season of overwhelming inspiration
is here at last.
My mind is flooded
with the carvings I will make,
the stories I will write,
the pictures I will paint...

In the dimly lit kitchen,
the stove squats lifeless,
waiting for the call to action.
The moment has come.
For the first time in months
I build a fire
in the chilled brick grate

and with a single match
the house is transformed.

Whispering my traditional toast
to "the heart of the home "
with a shot of malt whisky
in a small slipware cup,
the same simple cup used to toast my friends'
wedding
a few years ago in a small Scottish church,
always employed to celebrate the re-birth of the
stove.
I share a few drops with the flames
and feel the burn of the remainder
catch in my throat.
A small ritual act of reverence
important to me
though witnessed by me alone,
will always be marked.
This cup, the bond that will always bind
My dear friends' spirits
to my hearth
and my heart.

The old man and his dog

Together
Shuffling side by side
Old man and his companion
Old dog and his companion
Each to the other tied
Between them hangs a tether
Of faded, braided leather
Gently linking wrinkling, parchment hand
And collared neck
Together

the dell

There's a place along the track
that is without equal,
most blessed spot, balm to my heart
birthplace of myriad fantasies.

Close by, a rustic bench seat,
placed where the hedge is lowest,
offers views of bucolic near perfection
across the restless river
to luscious grassy meadows,
hemmed in by wooded hills.

A casual passer-by happening upon this spot
would likely take their ease here,
distracted by the verdant beauty
of the unfolding prospect.

But my spot is a few yards away,
where the babble and chatter of the gambolling
water
is muffled by the tree line.
The bank across the path
is high and rocky,
It's folded fissured slate
festooned with ferns and bearded with moss.

colossal ancient beech and oak
teeter precariously at the precipice rim

Now, in spring,
Improbably vivid acidic green shoots
force skywards
through musty skeletons of last year's fallen
leaves
Porcelain-white spectral fungi
gleam translucent on parchment-dry bark.

In summer
this haven becomes
a cool oasis of dappled shade,
where spiralling clusters of lace-winged insects
Swirl in hazy shafts
of filtered sunshine.

Autumn unfolds
And first a trickle,
then a cascade
of bright, crisp beech leaves
showering from a proscenium of vaulted
branches
casts a golden pallor over the whole stage
Crunching satisfyingly under foot.

When winter descends
A cathedral of towering silhouettes,

tormented by the wind,
scratch and claw against angry, slate grey skies

Badgers live here
powerful limbs tunneling deep in the loamy
bank.
Gaping setts, some between roots,
some part concealed beneath a tangle of
brambles,
all announced by a shining plateau
of dark umber earth
polished smooth by generations
of nocturnal perambulations.

But there's more

For here, in this dell
just around the corner from plain sight

there are faeries

For Freya. A lullaby

Just a tiny ripple
on an ocean vast and wide,
Barely even noticed
by the overwhelming tide.
Who knows what far-flung places
this little wave will reach,
Majestic, icy wastelands
or some warm exotic beach.

Just a little flutter,
a gentle summer breeze,
The lightest, freshest whisper
softly stirring in the trees,
brushing past the butterflies
and lifting up their wings
Shimmering on cobwebs
like tiny guitar strings.

Just a ray of sunshine
coaxing flowers into bloom,
subtly and silently
dispelling shady gloom.
Charming us, and teasing out
a smile from every face
Warming all she touches

with her innocent embrace.

She's just my little Princess,
not even two days old.
Like putty in her tiny fist,
my heart is hers to mould.
Already she has conquered me
and brought me to my knees
my ripple on the ocean
my warming summer breeze

daddy 16/7/08

Today the oak gave up her leaves

Today the Oak gave up her leaves.
The Cherry surrendered hers
almost before summer was out.
Long before the gales came
she was showering the byways with vivid reds
and golds.
The Ash too, weary of her labours,
divesting herself of her garments before they
even paled,
at the first hint of shortening days.
The lanes and hedgerows were blanketed in
discarded Ash leaves
almost overnight,
and the Ash was done with Autumn.
The others followed suit, some more gently
like the Sycamore who portioned out her fall,
so there might be a steady cascade of gold and
faded green
for days or weeks.
One by one the Aspen, Willow and Hazel turned
to russet and auburn,
so that when the frost came and the breeze
stiffened
they had no strength to resist.

As the breeze turned to wind
and the wind turned to a squall,
and the squall became a tempest,
the trees thrashed and bent and surrendered the
last of their leaves.
Those that tried in vain to hold on
had their leaves taken
and the branches that they clung to as well.
Alone in the valley the oaks still shone,
scarred but unbeaten by the tempest.
Leather brown leaves,
dry as old bones but still clinging on,
fluttering among the bare and broken limbs of
their neighbours.

This morning as I stepped out
on a day breathlessly still,
a gentle trickle of falling leaves
clattered through the hedge
and pattered on the road.
The stoic oak had alone withstood the savage
storm,
and now on a day so calm that a butterfly could
take wing,
the oak finally chose to return her leaves to the
soil.
Why today I just don't know.
This was simply the time of her choosing.

Decency lies broken

Decency lies bloodied and broken in the ditch
It seems the fight is finished, when a last convulsive twitch
Shudders through it's body, with a final rasping breath
It whispers "It's not over. I won't accept my death."
Set upon by those who would destroy democracy
with ignorance disguised as pride in keeping Britain free.

They think I'm done, they think they've won and taken all from me
When they refused diplomacy and spat on decency.

Be careful what you wish for, bully, If we have no choice
We will respond with all that's left, we'll find another voice.
You rely upon our discipline to fight within the rules
While you land blows below the belt and treat us all like fools.

But if the laws are tossed aside then we all fight
the same
And we will cast off all restraint when next we
play the game.
The playing field then leveled up, the weapons
drawn by all
You have not wit nor intellect to save you from
the fall.

For Susan

Love has been the raging torrent
that carved out the landscape of my life
And Susan was there,
in the pure virginal meadow of my youth,
the spring from whence that river grew.
I loved her with the totality that only a ten year
old boy can muster,
bewitched completely by her beauty and grace.
She was my world,
and the river began to shape and sculpt me.

Long summer afternoons playing
in her garden,
between high hedges that made this blessed
haven
a world apart,
private,
ours alone.

Holding hands
on a Sunday school trip
while we silently watched the sun hanging low
over a glass-still lake at the foot of the Mourne
Mountains.
The dizzying ecstatic thrill

Of her warm touch
pounding in my boyish chest
throbbing in my head
causing my dry breath to stutter….

In these moments
the poet and the artist in me were born,
sprung from an urgent need to express
the unbearable beauty of life.

In teenage years we briefly met again,
and again I offered up my heart to my muse
in an awkward adolescent way.
.

Innocently, and without malice or intent
she broke my heart.
Solace was sought in my first cheap wine and
cigarettes,
retreating to the shade of an Irish hedge
to punish myself
for hurting so much.

Alone again, back across the sea,
I discovered I excelled in this new-found
debauchery.
finding an unfamiliar kinship
in the company of other artistic souls,
dented and damaged by love and life.

Throughout my adult life,
when the world crushed my dreams,
I would fantasize that our worlds might collide
once more
in a scene from an old French movie
recapturing those moments of pure romance.
She was,
(though I never let on),
my emotional safety net.

But it was never destined for us.

Many years later we met again
for the last time.
Now both with families of our own,
we were happy.
Our rivers had taken different courses,
and hers had meandered through other lives,
bringing that same sweet smiling joy
to people I would never know.
For the first time in my life
I knew we were not marked down
For a future together.

And I smiled.

I was pleased for the love she had in her life,
for her faith,

for her family,
for all of those things
that she had found
and I had found
that would forever keep us apart.

We corresponded rarely now,
always with the safe warmth
of simple friendship
lending innocence to our exchange.

But Susan was my first muse

You never forget your first.

Her river no longer cascades……
But I still hear it's roar.
And the landscape it carved in my soul
in the very beginning
is forever my home.

Goodbye, "little blonde plaits"
I will never forget.
X

Enough

"Enough!" I cried,
"I've had enough
And I can do no more!"
As I scraped the drying rainbow
from the palette to the floor.
"My muse has just abandoned me,
her light is growing faint.
If I don't have her influence
then how am I to paint?"
I cast aside my brushes
and slumped into a chair.
Drained of inspiration,
and just

too

tired

to

care..

Snow

A confident sun eased itself, stretching, over the
horizon
basting with melted butter
the uppermost limbs of the trees in the valley.
A pledge of restorative warmth
to the stoic waxy holly
and encumbered viridian ivy.
Improbably bright flickers of light
flashed and glanced on frigid leaf and branch.
Long fingers of shadow
the colour of robins' eggs
reached out over the pale golden hillside across
the river.
Maybe today?
Then
a single dusty flake
then two....three....
a flurry......
And turning to face the stiffening breeze I saw it.
A featureless, towering, slate-grey wave
Looming over the virginal, cowering landscape
and breaking on the shoreline of scratchy bare
trees,
engulfing them in a swirling insistent smoke,
turning them to a muddy watercolour blur.
There would be no thaw

My girl

Feisty and sassy and tough as an eggshell
Vulnerable, sensitive, soft as an anvil
Things that would break me
she handles with ease
Things that don't matter
bring her to her knees
A harsh confrontation she'll take in her stride
But a misspoken word can make her run and
hide
 We are as different as peas in a pod
As much like each other as demons and Gods

She needs to be strong so I teach her to fight
But I also teach mercy, to do what is right.
I offer my knowledge, whatever that's worth
Endeavour to guide, as I have since her birth.

When she runs I will watch with a smile on my
face
When she walks I'll walk with her and try to
keep pace
When she falls I will catch her again and again
Wipe the blood from her knees, try to soften the
pain

Then she'll ride on my shoulders, 'til ready to
walk
Though my back may be aching
To where the road forks.

Then she'll make her decision and choose her
own way
Though tears steal my breath I won't ask her to
stay
So I'll set her back down, but I won't say
goodbye
I will watch from the sidelines, to be at her side
When she reaches the river, to build her a boat
When the cold chills her body, to give her my
coat.

And when all that is left is my breath on the
breeze
I'll whisper my love as I pass through the trees.

Platform

Stillness.
There is beauty in the calmness of the ordinary.
It is daylight now, but a quiet, understated dawn
that has not flushed the clouds with peach and
pink.
Colours are muted, there is barely a breeze.
The world is slow to wake at this time of year.
In this moment you can feel the history of a
place,
when the past sits close,
side by side with the present.
There are no loud colours to compete with,
so the faint shadows of long ago
can linger at the very edge of your sight.
There is no rustle of leaves in the wind to drown
out
the whispered echoes of forgotten conversations.
Here the roar of the river is distant, muted
and the silence lies as thick as fog
on the old railway line.
Looking back along the ruined remnants of the
platform,
with moss growing up and ivy hanging down,
with ferns bursting from between great granite
blocks,

and brambles choking doorless thresholds.
with drifts of slowly decaying, damp, dark
leaves
and fallen branches,
leaning like buttresses against roofless stone
pillars,
I can see them still,
The ghosts of the past.
Not menacing ghouls of common myth,
Not shrouded wraiths with sightless eyes,
pointing with skeletal fingers to warn of
impending doom.
These ghosts are but double exposures on the
film of time.
Ordinary men and women
who lived and worked
and dreamed and married
and died here,
and knew the rhythms of the weather and the
seasons of the year,
and were a part of this place.
They are still.
They know nothing of me,
for in their world I am as yet unborn.
Leaning against the quoin stones of the ruined
shed, a bearded man,
drawing on a pipe, enjoying the brief respite
before the next goods train arrives, demanding
to be loaded.

At the end of the platform, a callow youth
sits, swinging his legs over the edge,
ravenously devouring a huge pasty.
Another quiet man sits on a pile of dusty sacks,
carefully unwrapping an apple and some bread
and dripping
from a faded gingham cloth.
The bearded man cracks a joke, and all three
laugh,
the youth nearly choking on his lunch.
The others laugh even more.

From behind me, two incongruously corporeal
horse riders
clop slowly along the path.
I retreat into the hedge to let these denizens of
today pass
and across the track the whispering spirits on the
platform
fade into the ruins,
not able to compete with even the plodding
footfall of the horses
or the murmured conversation of the riders,
so faint has time rendered their voices.
They round the corner and are gone.
But the sun has now climbed high and the world
is waking.
Flecks of red and orange streak across the pale
blue sky .

Soon more people will come, with dogs and
conversations.
But the spirits will remain
not visible, but present,
and when next the world holds it's breath for
long enough
and the valley is still and deserted,
the smoke of the decades that masks these spirits
may thin just enough to hear that laughter from
long ago
once more.

Little Angel

High up in the rafters
On a creaking ancient bridge
The puppeteer stands silent in the shade
Hunched intently here he stands
Holding in his twitching hand
A wooden frame so intricately made.
From it, a web of slender lines
Suspend an angel carved from lime
Her features fixed forever in a smile.
And following the scripted page
She pirouettes across the stage
The captivated children to beguile.

Night after night she takes her place
To play her part with gentle grace
Her stoic dedication never wanes
This lovely little wooden girl
On silken strings will dance and whirl
And through it all she never once complains.

And what about the puppet man?
He's just assisting where he can he can.
He's happy on his bridge up out of sight.
Content to simply hold the strings
While Angel steps out from the wings
And dances once again before the lights.

Flute

With a sigh he sat,
rested his back against the willow
and closed his eyes.
The sun warmed his upturned face
and a light breeze teased the leaves above his
head.
From a waxed cloth bag he gently drew
a long slender flute of dark wood,
polished smooth by years of playing,
his fingers falling instinctively
onto the holes,
He lifted the flute to his thin, pursed lips
to play.
Soft, clear notes mingled with the babbling of
the stream
and the cry of the swallows high in the pale blue
sky.
His companions, a little way off, fell silent
and tilted their heads to listen.
The melody was strange and lilting,
not the raucous dance tune of a street performer,
but more the voice of the trees
singing the praise of the summer's warmth.
Soaring to a crescendo like birds in flight,
then cascading and tumbling to the meadow

and the cool shadows at the waterside.
Skipping and dancing among the buzzing
insects,
resting for a few moments on the wings of
butterflies
sunning themselves on the roses atop the hedge,
before flitting away again
to cavort among the swaying grasses in the
meadow.

But in his world the flautist was not alone.
Inside his head deep, sonorous base notes from
fat bellied instruments
rose from a foundation of quietly insistent,
resonant drums.
Branching melodies from violas and horns
stretched skywards.
Around them
and through each other
twisted a delicate shimmering latticework of
harmonies
from violins, mandolas, other flutes and pipes.
Behind his twitching eyelids
he nodded appreciatively to the musicians of his
youth,
smiling at the richness and fullness of the music
and the kinship
of the shared moment
known only to musicians.

In turn they took the lead from their fellows,
coming together again in soaring unity,
accompanying each other to a climactic finale
that faded away
like a sunset
to stillness.

But here on the riverbank
the travelers heard only the flute
and this, to them was beautiful enough.

Heron

Citrine the gaze that meets my own
Just for a heartbeat we are one
Then curtseying with balletic grace
It's snow cloud wings the air embrace
Beak, sharp as a bayonet
Slender head, and serpent neck
Sweep up and back, then with a spring,
The river barely rippling
As silver drips from scaly feet
To splash where shimmering water meets
Entangled roots and mossy bank
In silty pools and caverns dank .
The Steel Phoenix takes the air
And twists between the branches bare
Not a twig the wing tip brushes
Weaving deftly through the bushes
Out across the marshy plain
Master of this wild domain
Legs like jesses trail behind
Neck tucked tightly, serpentine

Shrugs away beyond the trees
With languid wingbeats, silently.
And as it's swallowed by the dawn
Bathed in light as gold as corn,

Stillness floods across the scene
As though the bird had never been.

The fall

While walking in the woods today
I came across, to my dismay
A great blue tree across the way
It's limbs all bent and broken.
It looked like a catastrophe
But on the bank, where once the tree
had stood, my happy eye could see
that something else had woken.
In amongst the churned up earth
A sturdy sapling, stout in girth
Was thrusting upwards from the earth
and glowing in the sunlight.
It's leaves all flushed with crimson hue
The red so warm against the blue
of the almighty titan, who
had fallen in the night.

Spirit Guide

Cruel passions cower just beneath
my tissue paper skin
I dare not touch the smallest thorn
The membrane is so thin.
If it should tear they will escape
And overwhelm my mind
Then, though I strain to see my path
I will again be blind.
And stumbling through the shadowlands
All lonely and alone
Barefoot I'll tread amongst the dead
Who can't find their way home.

But just when hope abandons me,
My heart engulfed by fog,
Here at my side,
my spirit guide,
My ever faithful
Dog.

A Pair of Irish Shillings

A pair of Irish shillings
From the year that I was born.
They're made up into cufflinks
But they've never yet been worn.
A three piece suit selected,
A herringbone affair.
It cost me half a fortune,
But I needed one to wear.
New shirt, new tie and braces,
And matching stockings too.
My shoes I thought were near enough
For they are nearly new.
I'm going up to Windsor,
To the castle I am bound,
To old St. George's College
That lies within the grounds.
For a glittering occasion
A wondrous thing to see
The kind of thing not normally
Accessible to me
For I've been nominated
An award might come my way
The Maker of the Year award
Given by the H.C.A.
A prestigious occasion

With a dress code to match
But here in Moss Bros changing room
I just looked up to catch
A sight of my reflection
Staring back out from the glass,
And I cannot help but wonder
Am I looking like an ass?

Trees....again

Collating this anthology
Of simple homespun poetry
It comes as no surprise to see
I write a lot about my trees.

But I make no apology
Those trees are very dear to me
And I don't know who I would be
Without my love of forestry

Read these words aloud with me
Before the mirror, you will see
That when you simply utter "tree"
You smile involuntarily